FOUNDATION
OF
Love and Hope

FOUNDATION
OF
Love and Hope

RUBY MERCER

*"The Lord is good, a strong hold in the day of trouble
And He knoweth them that trust in Him" (Nahum 1:7).*

XULON PRESS

Xulon Press
2301 Lucien Way #415
Maitland, FL 32751
407.339.4217
www.xulonpress.com

Unless otherwise indicated, Scripture quotations taken from the King James Version (KJV) – *public domain*.

Paperback ISBN-13: 978-1-66283-518-6
Ebook ISBN-13: 978-1-66283-519-3

I want to dedicate my book to:

My Lord and Savior first, for without Him I am nothing.

My husband, Troy. My Children, Kylie, Jessica, Anthony, Wendy, and Matthew.

My grandchildren, Jayden, Cassidy, Brantley, Charlie, and to my family and friends that believe and love me.

For God is our heavenly Father.

Inspirations can come in so many ways that at the time we don't realize it. One day, for example, you may be sitting around drinking a cup of coffee and start thinking about a song, a conversation, a friend, a pastor's sermon, a child's laughter, or maybe a billboard with a saying on it. There are no limits in which the Lord speaks to us, we just need to be still and listen to Him.

I want to share a little bit about where some of my inspirations came from in addition to the reasons. They may sound familiar to anyone that has suffered addiction, either in their family or even friends. Addiction is a slow crawling poison that will completely consume and destroy the addict as well as their loved ones either physically, emotionally, spiritually, and/or financially. I was at that point until I was at my last hope. Only the Lord knew it because I hid it, for I was broken to the point in which I could no longer fight. Satan thought he won, but my Savior took control. Praise God!

My son, daughter, and son-in-law were all active addicts at the time, and it certainly has been a whirlwind of a ride for eleven years. Hell on earth is the best way to describe it at times. I love my children with everything in me, but at times, "I didn't like them." My love for them would not let me stop praying for them. I believed and trusted that God would help them, but He wasn't doing it fast enough for me (I thought).

Then one morning, as I was on my way to work, I asked God, "WHY, Lord, am I having to go through this with my children? WHY? Lord, WHY? I try my best to help them but it doesn't help!" (Just remember when the Lord answers, He answers this way.)

It felt like a cinder block hit me in the head – it was His answer. "WHY, did I allow my son to go through what he did?" I responded with, "For you loved us and He died for all of us."

"Wow!" I exclaimed as I proceeded to ask him what I needed to do, but that answer came later that day, three times or some say confirmation. After lunch as I was sitting in the shade, I asked Him again, "What can I do Lord?" He answered when I turned the radio on. "Peace Be Still" came on and I said, "Okay, be still." I went on to my next job and there it was on a church sign again, "Be Still, Be Patient, Be Strong." This was my second confirmation, wow! I was thinking, "Be still Ruby."

On my way home from work, I saw a shirt with Psalm 46:10 on it that read, "Be still, and know that I am God: I will be exalted in the earth." I knew then without a doubt that God wanted me to be still and let Him move and work in my children.

I give God all the glory and praise for my children, for He has brought them through the storms of their past, and He will be with them in their future storms in life.

"Be strong and of a good courage,
fear not, nor be afraid of them:

For the Lord thy God, he it is that doth go with thee;
he will not fail thee, nor forsake thee" (Deu. 31:6).

I WANT TO GIVE THANKS
TO A VERY SPECIAL LADY,

Willie Mae Joyner:

A True Foundation of Love and Hope.

She's long since passed; however, her memory is still alive.

This is where my title came from, for she was a God fearing, humble, graceful lady that always admired and loved.

Rest in peace my friend.

"The Lord is good, a strong hold in the day of trouble; and he knoweth them that trust in him" (Na. 1:7).

"My Friend"

-Memory of My Inspiration-

She lived in all
Never wavered on her faith,
Loved her Savior,
Lived a humble life,
Loved unconditionally,
Smiled even in her sadness,
Never too tired to help others:
A Lady of Wisdom.
Who gave and asked for nothing in return;
Cherished her family and friends.
Her love will live forever,
The wisdom she shared:
Willie Mae Joyner
A True Foundation of Love.

"Wherefore comfort yourselves together
And edify one another, even as also ye do" (1 Thes. 5:11).

"The Vine"

We are the branch
Coming from the Vine.
We need the Vine,
For we need to branch out and grow.
Do not fear the drought,
For the Vine is full of nourishment.
Let the fruit of the Spirit feed you,
Our branches will sprout out
As we grow in the Holy Spirit
For the Vine is our Saviour:
Jesus Christ

"I am the vine, ye are the branches
He that abideth in me, and I in Him,
The same bringeth forth much fruit:
For without me, ye can do nothing" (John 15:5).

"Learn to Live"

Seek the Lord
In all things.
Go to God in Prayer:
Pray without ceasing,
Seek His Wisdom,
Ask for Guidance,
Live wisely in the Word.
Surround yourself with faithful Believers.
Pray for Peace in your soul,
Never give into failures
For God will turn them into success;
It's a part of growing in wisdom,
Let God light your pathway:
Learn to live in
"Trusting God".

"Seek the Lord and His
Strength, Seek His face
Continually" (1 Chro. 16:11).

"DANCE IN THE RAIN"

Let's dance in the Rain
While the wind blows;
Forget all the pain,
Let go of the care.
Dance in the Rain
While it soaks in my skin,
I will forget the Pain.
God's rain washes away my filth
I want to dance in the rain;
Splash in the puddles
Till' the thunder rolls in,
For God has forgiven me.
I want to dance in the rain
Till' the rainbow comes over.
I am not ashamed,
My Lord calls my name.
While I dance in the Rain,
He has washed away the shame
"Dancing in the Rain."

"Praise Him ye heavens of heavens,
and ye waters that be above the heavens" (Ps. 149:4).

"Find Your Peace"

Let your faith develop
As your trust grows
Trust in His word
Let go of the doubt
For His love is true
Let go of your worries
There He will give you hope
Start feeling the Joy
You thought was gone
Even in the troubles
His strength will help you overcome
You have found peace
In His presence.

"And he said, My presence shall go with thee,
And I will give thee rest" (Ex. 33:14).

"Strength"

In your dark hours
He's there for you
The enemy wants to destroy you
God can and will restore you
Don't feel ashamed
God knows you by name
If you feel weak
God's strength will carry you
If you are lost
God will light your way
What's destroyed in you
God will restore you fully
Take His hand
It's reaching for you
Let Him make you new
For His Love is true

"He giveth power to the faint; and to them
That have no might he increaseth strength" (Isa. 40:29).

"Past in the Past"

He was born in a nasty manger
He will go to your dark place
He was born in danger
Your area does not scare Him

Call for Him
Focus on your life
Just a call
You will never regret

Let your past be the past
Take His hand
Feel your future
Trust God's plan

Your past is over
Find your life
In the present
Of the Lord

"I sought the Lord, and He
Heard me, and delivered me
From all my fears" (Ps. 34:4).

"Victory through the Fire"

We may have trouble
God's priority is our Salvation
We may be lost
God's plan will come
Give it all to Him
Through the suffering
Our comfort will come
We will gain genuine Faith
Even Gold is put through the fire
Comes out Proved Pure
When Jesus wraps us up
It's our Faith
God will display His Victory

"But thanks be to God, which giveth us
The victory through our Lord Jesus Christ" (1 Cor. 15:57).

"Take A Stand"

Stand firm on the Rock
Never back down
Pray at all times
Go forward in His presence
Stand strong in His Word
Pray for strength
Overcome your weakness
Praise the Lord
In all things
Let your soul sing with Joy
Shout out to the Lord
Take a stand
Against the enemy
As a child of God
Being in His presence
Take a stand
Stand tall on the Rock
Strong in the Lord
"With the Living God."

"Jesus is the rock and
He is a firm place to stand
He is truth and His word is truth" (John 14:6).

"Worthy"

We are God's work
Created in His image
He loved us, before we were born
We were born in sin
Jesus went before us
He wore the crown of thorns
For our transgressions
The stripes from the leather straps
For our sins
He will never leave or forsake us
We can have peace
Knowing we are worthy
For our Savior
Will fight for you
For we are worthy

"For we are His workmanship, Created in Christ Jesus,
unto Good works, which God hath before Ordained that
we should walk in them" (Eph. 2:10).

"FOR ME"

As for me
I will call on the Lord
For I know He loves me
I will pray in the morning

For deliverance of my sins
He hears my prayers
I feel the presence
As I pray to Him in the evening

Pray for peace in my soul
My cries He hears
I pray at night
My soul rejoices with calmness

I cast my burdens on Him
For I belong to Him
He will not be shaken
For He has redeemed me

"As for me I will call Upon the Lord: and the Lord shall save me" (Ps. 55:16).

"Lost"

Little lost sheep
He didn't leave me alone
For I was wandering
He called my name

Satan was pulling me
I was lost
Satan didn't care
He loved my pain

The Lord called my name
I heard His voice
I reach for His hand
Jesus grabbed my hand

He saw me lost
Jesus left them all
To bring me back
To His flock

"My sheep hear my voice, and I know them, and they follow me" (John 10:27).

"Get up and Shout"

Shout loud
You're blessed
Praise His name
You're victorious
Praise the Lord
You will not be defeated
Shout to the Heavens
His word said it
I am a Believer
Shout it loud
For all to hear
His word will endure forever
My Savior is Alive
Get up and Shout
I have been set free

"Make a joyful noise unto the Lord, All the earth: make a loud noise, and Rejoice, sing praise" (Ps. 98:4).

"Seek Him"

In the dark tunnel
There's a light
Not that far away
You may be weak
Seek His strength
There' hope in the dark
Don't stray from the light
He is the light
Seek Him
Let Him gather you from
The darkness
He is a merciful God
He is our light in the dark
Have hope in Him

"The Lord is good unto them that wait For him, to the soul that seeketh him" (Lam. 3:25).

"Yes Lord"

I am blessed
From a sinner
To a believer
I was broken
Jesus put the pieces back together
I was lost in the forest
He found me and brought me out
I was sick in sin
He healed my body
I felt unloved
His love filled me
He is my Savior

"All that the Father giveth me Shall come to me; and him that cometh to me I will in no wise cast out" (John 6:37).

"TITUS 2:11 GRACE"

His Grace is for All
Bring salvation to All
Be Blessed
Not cursed
Live in Victory
Do not be defeated
Trust His word
Not man's word
Seek His will
Not the will of the world
God is Faithful
If you are tempted
He will show the way out
Trust His timing
Not your timing
For His word
Will endure forever

"For the grace of God that bringeth
Salvation hath appeared to all men" (Tit. 2:11).

"Invite them in"

Go to the streets
You can find the lost
See them on the corners
They're in full view
Share a meal
Share God's will
It's not a crime
To share some time
Invite them to the Lord's House
No matter their sin
Jesus died for all of us
He forgives all sin
Just invite them in
Let the Heavens rejoice
When they invite Jesus in
To forgive their sin

"O Magnify the Lord with me,
And let us exalt His name together" (Ps. 34:3).

"Trust in Him"

Seek the Lord's way
Not man's way
Have faith in Him
God is on your side
Even in our roughest days
God is always in control
We may think it's hard
He will make a way
Never give up
God is our strength
He lives inside us
For our love is in Him

"In God have I put my trust: I will not be Afraid what man can do unto me" (Ps. 56:11).

"Cling"

Hold to His promise
For it is true
Clinging to the truth
By His stripes I am healed
God's True Gift
Jesus Christ His Son
For He died on the cross
For our sins
The Lamb without blemish
For I am washed in the blood
I am cling to my sword
In the word of the Lord

"But ye that did cleave unto the Lord
Your God are alive every one of you this day" (Deu. 4:4).

"Don't Answer"

When the Past calls
Don't answer
It's enemy
He wants your future
Scream "Not Today!
Get thee behind me Satan!"
My past has been forgiven
It's a faded memory
That has been wiped away
God has set me free
For the Lord holds
The Key to my Future

"But he turned, and said unto Peter,
'Get thee behind me, Satan: thou art an offence
Unto me: for thou savourest not the things
That be of God, but those that be of men'" (Mat. 16:23).

"LET IT GO"

Worry will not help
Give it to God
It's okay to cry
Tears wash away the pain
Scream! Scream!
Feel better deep down
It's okay to live
It's okay to be happy
It's okay to relax
It's okay to let it go
For God is in control
Stand strong
Trust Him
Just let it go

"Being confident of this very thing,
That he which hath begun a good work in you
Will perform it until the day of Jesus Christ" (Phi. 1:6).

"He's moving 'You'"

Trust the move
Are you ready
"Be Still"
 God's moving
"Be Patient"
 God's moving
"Be Strong"
 God's moving
"Be Ready"
 God's moving
 Trust in the move
 For He's moving you

"And let us not be weary in well doing: For in due season we shall reap, If not we faint not" (Gal. 6:9).

Open the Door for Jesus
"New Beginning"

Open the front door
Ask God to come in
Invite the Holy Spirit
To roam freely in your home
Pray and Praise loudly to the Lord
Open the Back Door
Kick Satan right on outside
Praise the Lord
For the Lord Jesus Christ
Resides at this home
Forever more
Praise the Lord

"Then said Jesus unto them again,
'Verily, verily, I say unto you,
I am the door of the sheep'" (John 10:7).

"HIS FACE"

Lord I seek your face
Hear my cries
My soul aches
Have mercy Lord
I seek your way
Teach me Lord
Let faith and love
Take root in my soul
To grow in your word
As my body is weak
Strengthen me with your love
I seek you daily Lord

"Seek the Lord and his strength,
Seek his face continually" (1 Chr. 16:11).

"Living faithful"

Let the joy be seen in you
Share your love for God
Be at peace in all things
Your Patience comes from long suffering
Act and speak with gentleness
Seek and show goodness to all
Be faithful in your daily living
Let the Love of the Lord show in you
Speak with kindness
Share God's love

"Let us hold fast the profession of Our faith without wavering; (for he is For he is faithful that promised)" (Heb. 10:23).

"Storms to Sunshine"

Misery – The Dark Clouds
Finances – The Strong Winds
Depression – Sounds of Thunder
Anxiety – Pounding Rains
Life – A Storm of our Lives
Pray – This too Shall Pass
Savior – Seek Jesus Christ's Will
Healer – Calms the Storm
God – For He's Stronger than All Storms

"He maketh the storm a calm,
So that the waves thereof are still" (Ps. 107:29).

"Victory 'Claim It'"

Claim your Victory
Over your Troubles
Never waiver on your Victory
Stand on the Rock
Believe in the Victory
Have faith in the Victory
Watch the Lord's work
For your Victory

"Finally, my brethren, be strong in the Lord,
And in the power of His might" (Eph. 6:10).

"Start New"

He knows who you were
He knows who you can be
You see your weakness
He knows your strength

You feel like nothing
God knows something
You're a lost child,
God sees HIS child

You see the Old you
God will make you New
For He died for you
He loves you

"Therefore if any man be in Christ, He is a new creature, old things are passed away: Behold, all things are become new" (2 Cor. 5:17).

"Never Doubt"

Never doubt the Lord
For what He will do
If only we will be still
For His movement
Be Patient
It's His timing
Be strong
In His Word and Love

"Jesus answered and said unto them, 'Verily, I say unto you, If ye have faith, And doubt not, ye shall not only do this which is done by the fig tree, But also if ye shall say unto this mountain, Be thou removed, and be thou cast into the sea: It shall be done'" (Mat. 21:21).

"Trash the Sin"

Carry your sins to the Altar
And leave them there
Like a bag of trash
You carry out and leave
Leave the stink
Feel the fresh air
Rejoice and Praise God
He's got it from here

"Behold, for peace I had great bitterness;
But thou hast in love to my soul delivered it from the pit
of corruption: For thou hast all my sins behind thy back"
(Isa. 38:17).

"He's There with You"

There's no storm that
God will not be with you in
There's no bridge
God will not help you cross
There's no battle
God will not help you conquer
There's no problem
God will not help you solve
There's no place you're at
That God's not there
Don't be ashamed
Just call out His name

"Have not I commanded thee? Be strong and of good
courage; be not afraid, Neither be dismayed: For the Lord
thy God is with thee whithersoever thou goest" (Jos. 1:9).

"Nothing Lost"

Talk to God
No breathe is lost
Walk with God
You didn't walk alone
Wait on His time
His time will be the right time.
Read His word,
Grow closer to Him
Sing a song for Him
He doesn't mind if you're out of tune
Seek Him
He's easy to find
Trust in Him
He's already paid the cost
To keep you from being Lost

"And thou shalt know that thy tabernacle shall be in peace;
And thou shalt visit thy habitation, and shalt not sin"
(Job 5:24).

"My Armor of God"

"Help me keep it on"
Help me wear my belt of truth faithfully
Lord give me strength: When I am weak
Lord you are my shield in my fears
Tighten my shoes to walk in peace
For the conflict ahead of me
Secure my breastplate for the righteousness
Against all evil
Help me carry my sword to share your word

"But let us, who are of the day, be sober,
Putting on the breastplate of faith and love;
And for an helmet, the hope of salvation" (1 Thes.5:8).

"Love All"

Love them all
Pray for them
Jesus said love your enemies
As you love yourself
Love the ones who judge you
Find the good in others
Do not judge, accept them
For the Lord loves all
They may need a friend
We need to be kind
For troubles we all have
Humble and Kindness
May save them from pain
They may be part of
God's plans
For your future
Walk in the word

"'But I say unto you, Love your enemies, Bless them, that curse you, do good to them that hate you, And pray for them which despitefully use you, And persecute you;'" (Mat. 5:44).

"Choices We Make"

Choices we make daily
They will affect is the rest of our life
Pray before you make that choice
Pray for God's will and way
Entrust your choice in God's hands
That choice you will never regret

"Seasons from the Lord"

We are given seasons from the Lord:
Summer is for the enjoyment of walking
On the beach, hearing the waves washing
Upon the shore and rocks, finding seashells
Resting on the shore as they wash up from the depths below,
Playing in the pool with family and friends
While we wait patiently for the hotdogs
And hamburgers on the grill;
Memories of another summer come and go,
Those of which we can't get back, we have our
Photos, laughter, happiness, and love to cherish
For the season that's passed.

Fall comes for a new adventure of memories;
Changing of the leaves from bright colorful flowers to the rustic leaves:
Autumn leaves. The cool brisk wind blowing the leaves down to the ground
As Oysters roast by the fire with friends and family,
Talking about good times, planning a hunting trip.
Working on the river banks, fishing and watching the little ones catch
Their first fish and trying not to laugh
As they throw the pole down and run.
Sitting in the rocking chairs on the cool evening,
Drinking that fresh cup of coffee, watching the moon rise and stars appear.
Another season gone that we cannot get back; however,

We have our memories, photos, laughter, happiness, and love to cherish
For the season is gone.

Winter season comes: As we enjoy our warmth of our homes,
Catching snowflakes on our tongues, building a snowman
With friends and family, turning into a snowball fight,
Running inside cold and wet to be the first one by the fireplace to get warm.
Waiting on a cup of Hot Chocolate and smelling homemade soup
As it cooks on the stove.
Waiting on Santa Claus for the little ones to open their gifts,
To see their surprise and the gleam in their eyes.
Another season gone we cannot get back; however, we have our
Memories, photos, laughter, happiness, and love to cherish.
For the season is gone.

Springtime comes with beautiful,
Colorful flowers blooming; the birds chirping,
Butterflies floating from flower to flower.
Trees with the new green leaves making
Shade from the sun to sit under. Humming
Birds drinking from the feeders,
Squirrels chasing each other in the trees,
Hearing the sound of laughter as the little one's swing in the swings,
Riding down the dirt roads with the windows down
And hands hanging out of the window.
The bride getting ready to marry her soul mate

In the eyes of the Lord, friends, and family at the church
she grew up in.
Another season come and gone.
We have our memories, laughter, photos, and happiness
to cherish
For the season is gone.

We spend a lifetime of making memories,
Good and bad, Happy and sad.
Our life time is our season: rather it's a long or short season.
As humans we never want our loved one's season to
end on Earth.
We have to know our loved one's heavenly season will
never end;
And there will be no more pain, sickness, suffering and
loneliness.
So don't cry for them for your season has ended with them;
Instead, rejoice with memories, laughter, pictures,
love, and song.
Celebrate the season of life they shared,
For each one of us has our seasons on Earth.
Our everlasting season will be in our heavenly home
With our heavenly Father.

For the Lord knows when, where, and how long
Our seasons will last for we are to
Cherish each day. For when the Lord
Calls us home, our season on Earth will be a memory.
Don't cry, celebrate for I am enjoying my heavenly
home where
Seasons never end.

"And he said unto them, it is not for you to know the
times or the seasons,
Which the Father hath put in his own power" (Acts 1:7).

"Our Shelter"

Our pain
If it was like rain
The pain would ease off
Just like the heat after the rain
We could feel refreshed
Like the plants and grass
After a good rain shower
From the coolness of the rain
We could rest ourselves
And be at ease
Like the birds in their nest
After the rain
Only if pain was like rain
You can always take shelter
To get out of the rain
But with pain our only
Shelter is God
Call out to Him
He's our shelter in our pain

"The Lord is my rock, and my fortress, and my deliverer;
My God, my strength, in whom I will trust;
My buckler, and the horn of my salvation, and my high
tower" (Ps. 18:2).

"Battle, 'Be Like Moses'"

Raise your hands,
Raise your head,
Start leaning on the Lord.
Rise up
From your troubles,
Throw down your weaknesses.
Let go of the props,
Give God your downfalls,
Lean on Him,
Call on the Holy Spirit
To hold you up.
Be like Moses
He held his arms up
For the Lord's people crossed the Red Sea.
God wants us to win
Our battles.
Raise your hands in victory
For the battle has been won.

"And Caleb stilled the people before Moses,
And said, let us go up at once, and possess it;
For we are well able to overcome it" (Num. 13:30).

"I Give"

I give my life to you
I receive you as my Lord and Savior
You died for me
Your blood has covered me
I have been washed clean
Come into my life
Save me Lord
I seek your will
Let your light guide me
Lord, I am nothing
I ask you to make me
Something in your image
Praise the Lord
I am a child of the Most High
My Savior: Jesus Christ.

"For of him, and through him
And to him are all thing to whom
Be glory for ever Amen" (Rom. 11:36).

"10 Fingers"

1st Finger – Man
2nd Finger – A Crown of Thorns
3rd Finger – A Cross
4th Finger – Three Nails
5th Finger – The Father
6th Finger – The Son
7th Finger – The Holy Spirit
8th Finger – His Blood
9th Finger – The Tomb
10th Finger – Jesus descending to Heaven

This act of clasping your fingers together
To pray shows respect, humbleness, and communication
With our Lord and Savior.
We are requesting that Jesus hears and answers our prayers
And His will be done.

"Perfected"

I am not perfect
My savior is perfect
My behavior is not perfect
And he still loves me
I am not complete
My savior is complete
I make wrong decisions
Yet, He still loves me
I have been judged worldly
Only my Saviors' Judgement counts
I have been at fault
He still loves me
"Pilate" could not find fault
In my Lord
For He is Perfect
I am not Perfect
But by His grave
"I am being perfected"
When He "said"
It's complete "finished"
When He died for all

"To shew that the Lord is upright:
He is my rock, and there is no unrighteousness in him"
(Ps. 92:15).

"Plan of Salvation"

If you have not asked Jesus Christ
To come into your life and make you new in Him
And to save you from your sins,
Take a moment and pray to Him to forgive
You of your sins and make you new as a child of God
For you accept Him as your Lord and Savior
And that you believe in Him for He died for you.

"For God so loved the world, that he gave His only
begotten Son That whosoever believeth in Him should
not perish, but have everlasting life" (John 3:16).

Praise be to God, for ever and ever!

I am a firm believer in prayers. During this time of my emotional rollercoaster, I have found that a mother's love and prayer will be answered in God's timing, not ours. When a loved one drains you of your spiritual, emotional, and financial being, you begin to realize your love is not enough. God wants us to be still, be strong, be patient, and be happy. God's plans cannot be complete if we strive to do it ourselves. Over time, I have learned to stop and pray. Let it go, for God's time will be the right time. Ask Him to lift you of your burdens, and have complete faith and trust in Him. Never waiver, for He knows all, sees all, and can do all. Time is precious, but God loves each and every one of us. So much so that he allowed His only begotten Son, Jesus, to die on the cross for us. He loves us so deeply that everything in this world was created for us. We are His greatest creations. For a God who loves us so much, having faith is the greatest gift we can return. Give praise, and in return He will reward us openly. In the meantime, whilst waiting, enjoy your time on earth. Make the best of it, for this is only a temporary home. I, for one, am patiently waiting for what comes next.